E
612.8
S

Sarkisian, Kevin
You need your nose :
learning . . .

$11.50
BC#31210000374379

DATE DUE	BORROWER'S NAME
9/14/05	M quigley-Harris /c

E
612.8
S

BC#31210000374379 $11.50
Sarkisian, Kevin
You need your nose :
learning . . .

Connally Elementary School

PowerPhonics™

You Need Your Nose

Learning the N Sound

Kevin Sarkisian

The Rosen Publishing Group's
PowerKids Press™
New York

It is nice to have a nose.

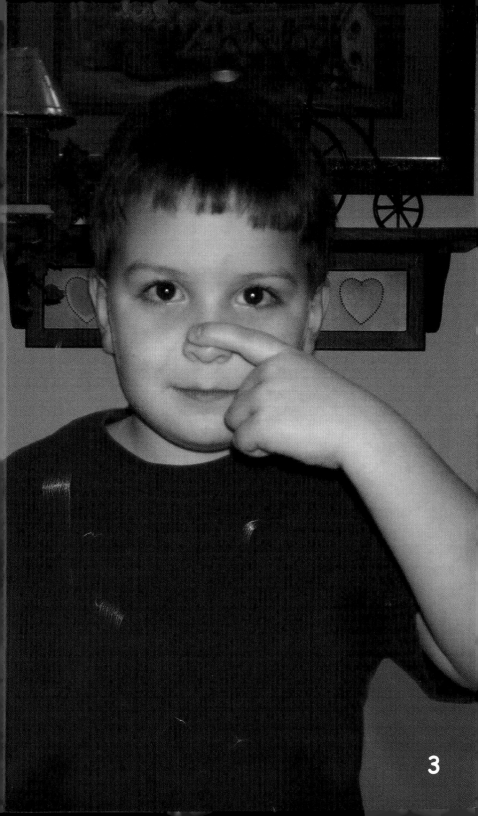

You need your nose to smell things.

You need your nose to smell a flower.

You need your nose to smell grass.

You need your nose to smell a pie.

You need your nose to smell a cake.

You need your nose to smell cookies.

You need your nose to smell popcorn.

You need your nose to smell pizza, too.

19

Noses are neat!

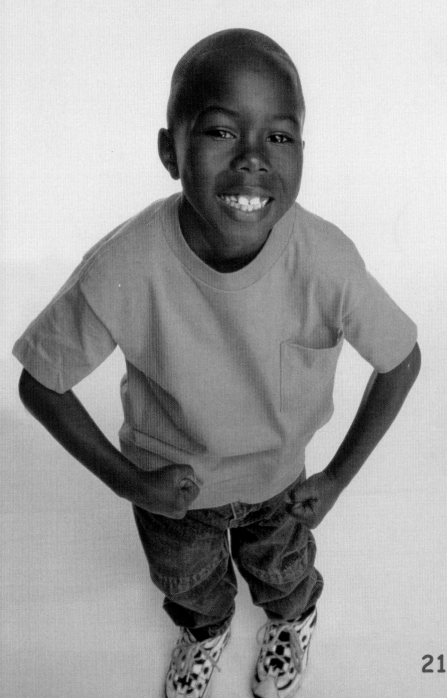

Word List

neat

need

nice

nose

Instructional Guide

Note to Instructors:
One of the essential skills that enable a young child to read is the ability to associate letter-sound symbols and blend these sounds to form words. Phonics instruction can teach children a system that will help them decode unfamiliar words and, in turn, enhance their word-recognition skills. We offer a phonics-based series of books that are easy to read and understand. Each book pairs words and pictures that reinforce specific phonetic sounds in a logical sequence. Topics are based on curriculum goals appropriate for early readers in the areas of science, social studies, and health.

Letter/Sound: n – On a chalkboard or dry-erase board, draw stick figures of a boy and a girl. Label them *Nick* and *Nancy*. Have the child listen for words that begin with the same sound as Nick and Nancy's names in the following sentence: *Nick and Nancy noticed that the date on the calendar was November ninth.* List initial consonant **n** words as the child gives them. Talk about why some words have capital **N**.
- Have the child give initial **n** words that rhyme with the following: *map, soon, eat, boys, game, best, poodle, pail, lumber, purse, rose, pine, pickle, go, cow, mice, seed,* etc. Write the child's responses on the chalkboard or dry-erase board. Have them underline the initial **n** in each word.

Phonics Activities: Have the child think of initial **n** words in response to the following clues: someone who works in a hospital, a month in the fall, time for lunch, the opposite of quiet, what 8 + 1 equals. List the child's responses on the chalkboard or dry-erase board. Have them underline the initial **n** in each word.
- Have the child decode the following one-syllable words: *get, map, hot, sick, hip, best.* Have the child form new words by substituting **n** for the initial consonant in each word.
- Make two columns on the chalkboard or dry-erase board, one labeled *m* and the other labeled *n*. Have the child read the following descriptive words as you list them: *neat, messy, new, noisy, many, nine, muddy, nearby, mild.* Ask the child to think of naming words that start with **n** or **m** (*nurse, nest, nickel, monkey, mop, map,* etc.). Have the child create phrases by combining each descriptive word with a naming word having the same initial consonant sound. (Examples: *neat nurses, many monkeys, nine nests,* etc.)

Additional Resources:
- Cobb, Vicki. *Follow Your Nose: Discover Your Sense of Smell.* Brookfield, CT: Millbrook Press, Inc., 2000.
- Frost, Helen. *Smelling.* Mankato, MN: Capstone Press, Inc., 2000.

Published in 2002 by The Rosen Publishing Group, Inc.
29 East 21st Street, New York, NY 10010

Book Design: Ron A. Churley

Photo Credits: Cover © Michael Goldman/FPG International; p. 3 by Ron A. Churley; p. 5 © Ross Whitaker/Image Bank; p. 7 © Jim Cummings/FPG International; p. 9 © Dusty Willison/International Stock; p. 11 © Image Port/Index Stock; p. 13 © Bob Daemmrich/Stock, Boston/Picture Quest; p. 15 © Michael Newman/PhotoEdit/Picture Quest; p. 17 © SW Production/ Index Stock; p. 19 © Dana White/PhotoEdit/Picture Quest; p. 21 © Bill Tucker/ International Stock.

Library of Congress Cataloging-in-Publication Data

Sarkisian, Kevin.
    You need your nose : learning the N sound / Kevin Sarkisian.
        p. cm. — (Power phonics/phonics for the real world)
    ISBN 0-8239-5910-4 (lib. bdg.)
    ISBN 0-8239-8255-6 (pbk.)
    6-pack ISBN 0-8239-9223-3
    1. Nose—Juvenile literature. 2. Smell—Juvenile literature.
    [1. Nose. 2. Smell.]   I. Title. II. Series.
    QP458 .S27 2001
    612.8'6—dc21
                                        00-013159

Manufactured in the United States of America